P9-CQS-613

DEC 2 1 2011

WITHDRAWN
CLARK PLEASANT BRANCH

Johnson County Public Library
401 State Street
Franklin, IN 46131

DEMCO

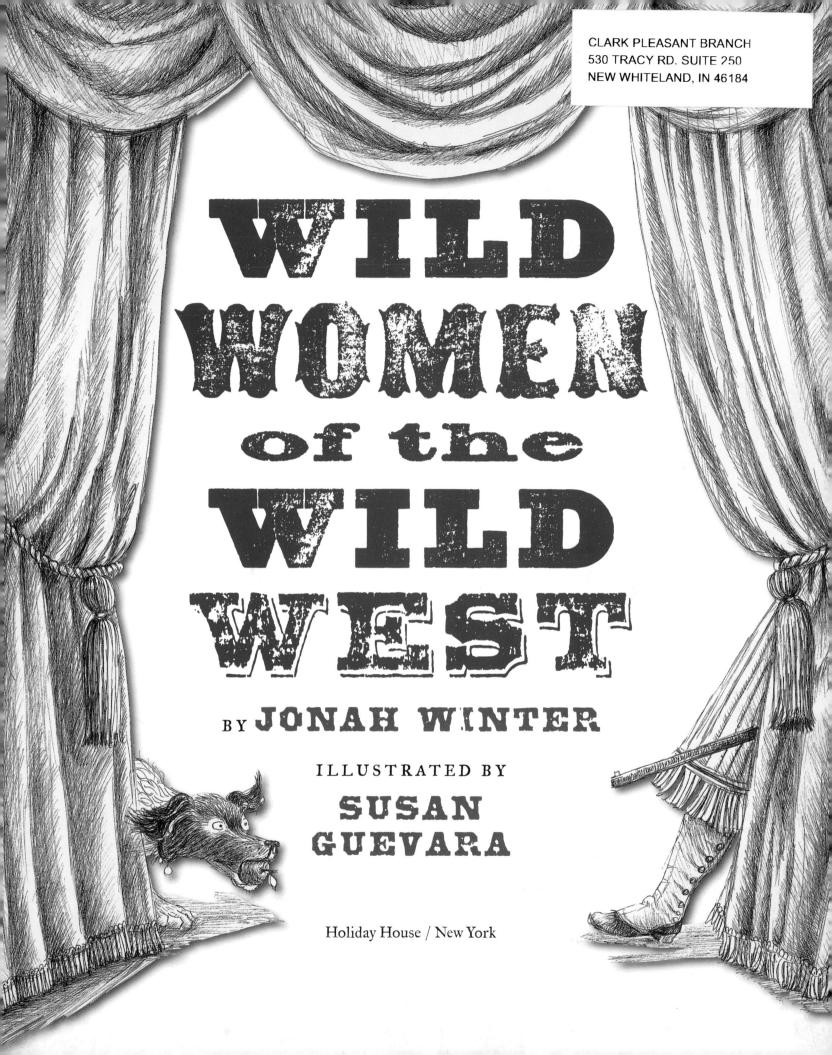

CLARK PLEASANT BRANCH
530 TRACY RD. SUITE 250
NEW WHITELAND, IN 46184

WILD WOMEN of the WILD WEST

BY JONAH WINTER

ILLUSTRATED BY

SUSAN GUEVARA

Holiday House / New York

Text copyright © 2011 by Jonah Winter
Illustrations copyright © 2011 by Susan Guevara
All Rights Reserved

HOLIDAY HOUSE is registered
in the U.S. Patent and Trademark Office.
Printed and Bound in July 2011 at Tien Wah Press,
Johor Bahru, Johor, Malaysia.
The text typeface is Fell.
The artwork was created with watercolor,
crow quill pen, and permanent ink pen.
www.holidayhouse.com
First Edition
1 3 5 7 9 10 8 6 4 2

Library of Congress Cataloging-in-Publication Data
Winter, Jonah, 1962-
Wild women of the Wild West / by Jonah Winter ; illustrated by Susan Guevara. — 1st ed.
p. cm.
Includes bibliographical references.
ISBN 978-0-8234-1601-1 (hardcover)
1. Women pioneers—West (U.S.)—History—19th century—Juvenile literature.
2. Frontier and pioneer life—West (U.S.)—Juvenile literature.
3. West (U.S.)—History—19th century—Juvenile literature.
4. West (U.S.)—Social life and customs—Juvenile literature.
5. Women pioneers—West (U.S.)—Biography—Juvenile literature.
6. West (U.S.)—Biography—Juvenile literature.
7. Women—Biography—Juvenile literature.
I. Guevara, Susan, ill. II. Title.
F596.W63 2011
920.720978—dc22
2010030911

Contents

✳ **Wild!** ✳

Not that long ago, there was a time when cowboys and gunfighters rode through the streets. People shot their guns in the air—and even at each other—in the western United States. No one knew exactly who was in charge. It was called the "Wild West." It was wild!

There weren't too many women in the Wild West, so the few who were there had to be really wild to compete with all those raucous men. There were all sorts of ways for the women to be wild. Belle Starr was an outlaw. Lola Montez did crazy dance routines for crowds of rowdy gold miners. Mary Fields drove stagecoaches in Montana and stood up to men who crossed her. On the other hand, Esther Morris did her fighting inside the courthouse—as the first woman judge. Nellie Cashman went to remote parts of the Yukon Territory to mine for gold—and she struck it rich cooking steaks. Yee-haw!

This all happened during a brief period of time. It all started with the California gold rush in 1849. Suddenly the population of the West exploded. Everyone wanted to go there. It took a while for things to settle down, but not that long. Much of the West was tame by the early 1890s.

By 1893, the last of the transcontinental railroads, the Great Northern Railway, had been completed. Also, most of the gold and silver that had lured so many folks had been mined by this time. Most of the outlaws who had put the "wild" in Wild West were either dead or in jail. And the fighting between whites and American Indians was pretty much over. It wasn't until 1898, though, that the Wild West was officially finished. That was the year of the Klondike gold rush, the last of the gold rushes. That extended the wildness and the frontier to their northern limits.

The geographical boundaries of the Wild West are a little fuzzy. Everyone can agree that the Pacific Ocean forms the western boundary. That's easy. And most would also agree that the Wild West was bordered by Canada on the north and the eastern borders of Minnesota, Iowa, Missouri, Oklahoma, and Texas on the east.

The northern border between Mexico and California is generally designated as the southern border of the Wild West. However, many would argue that Mexico was definitely a part of the Wild West. In many ways, the spirit of the Wild West lived on in Mexico long after it had officially ended in America: the lawlessness, the vitality, the preindustrial society.

Whether north or south of the Mexican border, the women who roughed it in the Wild West were some of the bravest people in the world. They proved that you don't have to be a man to be wild—not that this fact should need proving. Yippee tie yie yoe!

Calamity Jane

[1852–1903] ★ *Bull Whacker*

When people think of wild women of the Wild West, usually the first woman they think of is Calamity Jane. Calamity Jane was both wild and Western. She did all sorts of wild things that ladies didn't normally do, even back in the days of the Wild West:

- She used curse words when she talked.
- She chewed tobacco—and spit it.
- She carried a big gun, which she shot at things and people.
- And she wore men's clothes—for example, trousers.

Calamity Jane had been wearing trousers long before she was "Calamity Jane." When she was born, her parents gave her the name Martha Jane Canary. Then they died, leaving her all alone in the wild state of Montana. She was only sixteen, afoot in a field of gun-toting men. To survive, she disguised herself as a boy so she could get tougher jobs.

Her first job was on the transcontinental railroad, which would not hire women. All the men and boys she worked with thought she was one of them—until one day at the swimming hole. Discovered to be a girl, she was fired.

Her next job was as a mule skinner. A mule skinner was not someone who took the skin off a mule. A mule skinner, or "bull whacker," was a person who drove a team of animals, usually oxen or mules, with a whip. It was hard work. Most men could not handle such sweaty, back-breaking labor. But Calamity Jane did, and she didn't even have to wear a disguise.

According to Calamity Jane's own version of her story, she also fought in the army with General Custer. That was in addition to driving stagecoaches, prospecting for gold, working for the Pony Express, and nursing wounded soldiers on the battlefield. That's what she says in her book, *The Life and Times of Calamity Jane by Herself.*

Other accounts confirm that she really did work in the army as a scout. She also lived in a lot of places, rambling from one town to the next searching for work and adventure.

She finally wound up in a town named Deadwood in South Dakota. There she met the love of her life, Wild Bill Hickock. Calamity Jane said that they were married by a preacher on horseback.

Like Wild Bill Hickock, Buffalo Bill, and other wild men of the Wild West, Calamity Jane is half myth and half truth. Part of the myth comes from the dime novels written about her by a man named Ed Wheeler. He wrote a series of Western adventure novels about "Deadwood Dick" and Calamity Jane that helped to turn her into a legend. Whether it's all true or not, the story of Calamity Jane reinvented what it was to be a woman.

Mary Fields

[1832–1914] ★ *Stagecoach Driver*

Mary Fields was also called Stagecoach Mary. She got that name from being a stagecoach driver in Montana. Stagecoach driving was not only hard work, it was dangerous. Masked bandits with six-shooters might be hiding behind any rock or cactus waiting to rob stagecoaches—or worse. But was Stagecoach Mary scared? Nah. The robbers were probably more scared of her!

Mary was six feet tall and built like a brick house: big-boned and muscular. She got that way from plowing fields as a slave. Mary Fields was born into slavery in Tennessee. But even as a little girl, Mary was strong and tough. She could beat any boy in a fight, and she could refuse to do work. Most slaves got whipped for such behavior, but Mary seemed to have a strange power over everyone who crossed her path, and nobody bossed her around too much.

After the Civil War had ended and slavery was abolished, Mary stayed on as a worker at the same plantation. By this time, she smoked cigars, dressed like a man, and hung out with some rough characters.

When the plantation went out of business, fifty-year-old Mary Fields was hired at a convent in Montana. Her job was to haul stones, lumber, and grain and to supervise men. She was said to weigh two hundred pounds, wear a cowboy hat, and sport a couple of Colt 45s. She must have looked like someone you wouldn't want to mess with.

Oh, but one unfortunate cowboy did mess with her. He told her he wouldn't take orders from a woman, especially from a black woman. She repeated her orders. The man knocked her down. She challenged him to a gunfight and won.

The good news was, the man survived. The bad news was, Mary Fields lost her job at the convent. The nuns could not have a gunfighter working in a house of God. Mary's next job would make her famous: as a driver of a stagecoach for the U.S. Postal Service.

She was sixty years old when she began. And she was only the second woman to work for the U.S. Postal Service. That was in 1892. Cracking her bullwhip, firing her guns in the air, hooting and hollering, Stagecoach Mary drove that stagecoach through lawless land for eight years—until she was sixty-eight!

By that time it was 1900, and the Wild West was pretty much tamed—but not Mary Fields. Until her last days, Mary could be seen at the local saloon in Cascade, Montana, drinking beer, smoking cigars, and talking tough. She was one woman who would not be bossed around. She was a living example of what the Wild West stood for: freedom!

Mary Elizabeth Lease

[1830?–1933] ★ *Public Speaker*

You can use stagecoaches and firearms to express yourself—and you can use words. That's what Mary Elizabeth Lease did. She was the most famous public speaker of the Wild West. She gave loud speeches to very large audiences of mainly farmers.

It all started when Mary was just sixteen years old in Pennsylvania. Being very smart, she had already landed a teaching job. And being very feisty, she already had something she wanted to speak out against: low wages paid to teachers. She organized a movement to demand higher wages. When it did not succeed, she set out for the land of individuality and personal freedom: the West. One of the first things Mary Lease did in the West was get married. That was in Kansas. Next came many years of a hard, boring life. The government gave people land called homesteads to farm. Mary and her new husband had a hard time homesteading.

For one thing, the government gave them dry, poor land. Like most other Kansas homesteaders, Mary and her husband were poor themselves. Banks cheated them. The railroad companies swindled them, charging too much to ship their crops. Then came the great Grasshopper Epidemic of 1874. Mary and her family lived in a ditch because they couldn't afford a house. In the winter, they had to use buffalo chips for fuel. There were no trees. They had no friends.

These experiences shaped Mary Elizabeth Lease and her speeches years later. Through much hard work, she became a lawyer and then a public speaker in Wichita, Kansas. She was so good at speaking that people asked her to give speeches everywhere. She spoke mainly about women's rights and farmers' rights. Her speeches were filled with passion.

She spoke in a deep, booming voice that mesmerized the audience. Part of her power came from her looks, too. She was tall, thin, and pale, and wore all black. She had a sharp nose and thin lips, with a very high forehead. It was hard to ignore someone who looked like this, especially since her voice was hypnotic and she was saying intelligent things.

In the 1880s, Mary Lease was a leading light in a political movement called populism. Populists encouraged farmers and all poor people to fight the government and big business. Mary was a public speaker for two populist parties between 1890 and 1894: the Farmers' Alliance and the People's Party. Altogether, she gave one hundred and sixty speeches for the populist movement in Kansas.

Her most famous quote was: "You farmers ought to raise less corn and more hell." And the farmers followed her advice. When Mary Elizabeth Lease talked, people listened. In the Wild West, she was a legendary speaker. In a different era, she might have been a presidential candidate.

Lola Montez

[1819?–1861] ★ *Entertainer*

The gold rush happened in 1849 all of a sudden. Someone discovered gold in the mountains of California and then, BOOM!, men just flowed into the state with a pan and a dream. There were doctors, hobos, lobstermen, businessmen, artists, carpenters, theatrical managers, you name it—all hoping to strike it rich.

The problem was, there were hardly any women. Many of the gold miners were husbands who had left their wives back East. So, for the most part, these poor miners had only one another for company.

That's where Lola Montez fit in. Lola Montez was the most beautiful woman many gold miners had ever seen. She was not the most talented dancer or actress in the world, but she made up for this with her eccentricity. She was fun to watch.

Picture, if you will, the roughest makeshift theater. Just a few boards are nailed together for a stage. There are no velvet curtains, just some dirty sheets. There's just a dirt floor for the audience. Then who should appear but a mysterious woman dressed in the finest French clothes, with black hair and deep blue eyes, and a beautiful name: Lola Montez. She won the hearts of rowdy miners from one gold rush town to the next with a thing she called the "Spider Dance."

The Spider Dance was a wild dance routine Lola Montez had invented. It involved spiders—well, actually, they were just fake spiders suspended from invisible threads. She danced around with them for a while, then she pretended they were trying to bite her. Dropping the spiders, she whirled around and around, stomping madly and flouncing her petticoats. It was quite a sight!

And to think, this wild Western woman was a countess from Europe! Her official title was the Countess of Landsfeld. Landsfeld was in Bavaria, which is now in Germany. Lola was friends with the king of Bavaria, who made her a countess. She also knew famous artists, composers, and writers, like Franz Liszt, Victor Hugo, and George Sand. Lola claimed that the English poet Lord Byron was her father and that her mother was Spanish. She had invented her own name. No one knew for sure who she really was, and Lola like it that way.

For a few years in the early 1850s, Lola was the talk of the town. She was the center of attention in San Francisco and gold rush towns such as Rough and Ready, You Bet, and Grass Valley, where she owned a house. During her heyday, she walked a bear on a leash through the streets of her other home, San Francisco. And to this day, San Francisco continues to be the home of many free-spirited individuals like Lola in whom the wildness of the Wild West lives on.

Lotta Crabtree

[1847–1924] ★ *Entertainer*

At the same time that Lola Montez lived in Grass Valley, there was a little girl there named Lotta Crabtree. Lola liked Lotta, and Lotta worshipped Lola. She loved how Lola was able to hold an audience's attention. So Lotta tried performing herself. She did really good impersonations of local people that caused all the grown-ups to laugh. She did a dance routine in the blacksmith shop. Before you knew it, she was onstage.

And she was only eight years old! Lotta Crabtree was not the first or only child star of the gold rush, but she was the most famous. Audiences loved her, and newspaper writers loved her.

Lotta made people laugh. The roles she played involved lots of physical humor. She would wink really big and make all sorts of funny faces. Then she would wiggle around the stage and kick up her legs a lot. Before there were the Three Stooges or Shirley Temple, there was Lotta Crabtree.

She danced jigs, sang songs, played the banjo, acted in plays, and did comedy routines. Wherever she went, from the mining towns to San Francisco and, later, across the whole country, Lotta brought waves of nostalgia and tears of laughter to the hearts and eyes of her audiences.

Though Lola Montez and Lotta Crabtree were both gold rush entertainers and good friends, they were like night and day. Lola Montez appealed to the forty-niners' hunger for wild adventure. Lotta Crabtree made them remember, tearfully, the children and the innocence they had left behind.

Doña Maria Gertrudis "La Tules" Barcelo

[1800–1852] ★ *Casino Owner*

One of the wildest things about the Wild West is that it had another name just a few years before the California gold rush. It was called Mexico. In the early 1800s, Mexico owned much of what is now the western United States: Texas, Arizona, California, Nevada—all the way up to the Montana border!

That's why a lot of the names of Western cities and states are Spanish, such as San Francisco, San Antonio, Las Vegas, and Colorado—they were once all part of Mexico. One of the most prosperous towns of *norteño*, or northern Mexico, was Santa Fe. Because of the Santa Fe Trail, which stretched from Santa Fe (in what is now New Mexico) to Missouri, Santa Fe was a busy crossroads. There were all sorts of people passing through Santa Fe all the time: Mexicans, Anglo Americans, and other foreigners. The visitors danced, ate well, and gambled. They especially loved to gamble.

The most popular place to gamble in Old Santa Fe belonged to a woman known as La Tules. Her full name was Doña Maria Gertrudis Barcelo; and during the 1830s and '40s, she ruled the Santa Fe nightlife. She was a monte dealer.

Monte is a card game played against a dealer for money. As long as monte has been a game, gamblers have usually lost to the dealer. But losing to someone as beautiful and charming as La Tules didn't feel so bad!

Señora Barcelo did her first monte dealing in 1825 outside Santa Fe. She had escaped from an unpleasant marriage in Old Mexico and had made her way to frontier country in New Mexico. It took a lot of nerve to leave her husband and start a new life all alone in a far-off place. But nerve was what made Barcelo such a good monte dealer and such a good businesswoman.

By the 1830s, she had made enough money to open her own beautiful casino and hotel in the fanciest section of Santa Fe, in the downtown plaza. By the 1840s, her establishment was known far and wide as the place to go if you wanted a game of monte.

Her casino was so popular, in fact, that when the Mexican-American War started in 1846, Barcelo decided to stay. Even though many of her friends were fleeing back into Old Mexico, she was not about to abandon a successful business. Her casino became the favorite hot spot for American soldiers during the war, which lasted from 1846 to 1848. She became good friends with the Americans and even lent money to the United States Army during this period. When America won the war and annexed New Mexico, Ms. Barcelo was sitting pretty.

By the time she died in 1852, La Tules had amassed a sizable fortune. She had achieved things that many Americans would not have expected of a Mexican woman. She had been a political adviser to both the Mexican governor, Armijo, and to the United States government. She once warned the U.S. of a planned massacre of Americans by the Mexican Army. And, according to her wishes, she had one of the largest, fanciest funerals in Santa Fe history.

Señora Barcelo was only one of many Mexicans who influenced the West. Mexico gave us the cowboy, cowboy boots, guitars, beans, barbecue—practically everything we think of as "Western." Most of all, Mexico brought us and continues to bring us Mexicans, whose increasing presence in the West may once again make Spanish that region's first language.

Annie Oakley

[1860–1926] ★ *Sharpshooter*

Annie Oakley was called Little Sure Shot because:

- she was little, and
- she was a sure shot.

No woman had ever been as skilled with a gun as Annie Oakley. She could shoot a gun better than any man in the Wild West. She didn't get into gunfights, though; she got into contests: sharpshooting contests.

In her first big contest, she beat a famous sharpshooter named Frank Butler. Then, goll durn, she married him! The two of them were asked by Buffalo Bill to join his traveling Wild West Show. They agreed. Soon Annie Oakley became the main attraction.

The Wild West Show was like a traveling circus starring real-life legends of the Wild West. There was Sitting Bull, the famous Lakota chief. There was of course Buffalo Bill himself, the most famous Pony Express rider of the Wild West. And there was the most Wild Westerner named Bill of them all: Wild Bill Hickock. He tried circus life for a while but then headed back to the prairie.

You see, the Wild West still existed in 1883 when the Wild West Show first pitched its tent. Even as the Wild West Show traveled from town to town, around the country and the world, cowboys were still shooting it out on dusty streets and falling off real balconies. Buffalo Bill's show was something for wild men and women to do after they had retired from real wildness.

Annie Oakley, whose real name was Phoebe Anne Oakley Mozee, was not from the West herself. Nor was she all that wild in real life. She was kind of quiet. But beneath the big top, every night:

- she shot apples off her dog's head
- she shot glass balls behind her, over her shoulder, using a mirror
- she shot clay pigeons in midair while leaping off a mobile horse
- she even shot the heart out of the ace of hearts!

Without ever living in the Wild West, Annie Oakley became its most famous woman. Besides being the best sharpshooter of all time, she stood for something very important in the Wild West: the freedom of a person to be anything she or he darn well pleased.

Belle Starr

[1848–1889] ★ *Outlaw*

Belle Starr is the most famous woman outlaw of the Wild West. Two of the names she has been called are the Lady Desperado and Queen of the Bandits. She looked and acted like a queen—even though she was mainly just a horse thief.

While Belle Starr was stealing horses, she wore a long velvet dress and plumed hat. Once upon a time when she was a girl, Myra Belle Shirley had learned Latin, Greek, and Hebrew. She had learned how to play the piano, too. As an adult, she carried herself upright, with the dignity befitting a refined lady. She carried a gun, too, but she didn't really shoot people with it. She just stole their horses—usually when they weren't looking.

Horse thievery seemed to be a family tradition. Belle's brother got killed stealing horses in Texas. And speaking of Texas, that's where Belle was living when her first outlaw husband, Jim Reed, got killed during a robbery. Her second husband, Bruce Younger, was an outlaw as well.

Her third husband was the famous Cherokee outlaw Sam Starr. They lived in Indian Territory, or Oklahoma as it's now called—where she and Sam were arrested in 1882 for horse thievery.

The place where Belle and Sam lived was called the Robbers' Roost since it was used as a hide-out for various outlaws on the run. Also, according to legend, it was the home base for a gang of thieves led by Belle herself.

There are a lot of stories about Belle Starr that are probably made up. For instance, she was supposed to have been a member of a gang run by Jesse James and Cole Younger, two famous outlaws. Some people called Belle Starr the "female Jesse James." She was supposed to have been a bank robber, a train robber, and a murderer. She was supposed to have been a spy for the Confederate army.

Growing up as she did in Missouri, it's possible that Belle did help the Confederate army. Missouri was a big battleground between the Union and the Rebels during the Civil War. Her brother Bud was a Confederate killed by Union troops. Maybe that's why Belle became an outlaw.

What other things Belle Starr did may never be known. But she must have really been something to have earned the title the Petticoat Terror of the Plains.

Polly Pry

[1857–1938] ★ *Reporter*

Polly Pry was the nice, short name used by Leonel Ross Campbell when she did her newspaper reporting. Her articles made her the most famous lady reporter in the Wild West.

She started reporting in New York City, where she wrote about things that happened in dangerous neighborhoods. Her first job reporting in the West was in Denver. She wrote about mining disasters, a cannibal, and insane asylums. She went places where her life was in danger. She wrote things that angered people. She received threats on her life. One time, a guy showed up at her door and shot at her.

Luckily, he missed.

At first, not even her fellow reporters liked her. Who was this beautiful woman parading around the office like she owned the place? Was she a real reporter? These men found out in no time that she was, and she gained their respect.

In fact, two men who ran the newspaper, *The Denver Post,* owed their lives to Polly Pry. She tackled a gunman who was trying to shoot her two bosses in the newsroom. She grabbed at the gun, and she said something like "Go ahead, shoot me. Then you'll be sentenced to death." The gunman ran away. Her bosses lived. She was a hero.

No woman before her had ever worked for *The Denver Post.* When Polly Pry moved to Colorado in the 1890s, there were hardly any women working on any newspapers in the West. She was a pioneer, and a tough one at that. She was assigned the hardest, most dangerous stories.

Her last story for *The Denver Post* was about some mysterious murders that had taken place in various mines. Because women weren't allowed in mines back then, she had to disguise herself as a man to enter them.

Once inside the mines, she took notes on the horrible working conditions. She wrote a series of articles that got her—and *The Denver Post*—in BIG trouble. The men who owned the mines were very rich and powerful . . . and angry. Polly Pry was fired.

After that, Polly Pry simply started her own publication called . . . *Polly Pry*! In it she wrote about whatever she darn well pleased.

Long after the Wild West was no longer wild, Polly Pry kept putting herself in the most dangerous situations around the world and writing about them. She was one courageous—and wild—woman.

Sarah Winnemucca

[1844–1891] ★ *American Indian Leader*

During the time of the Wild West, the United States Army was sending soldiers West to kill American Indians and force them onto tiny reservations. In the 1800s, many white people thought of American Indians as not even human—as "savages"! Seeing them this way helped the invading whites steal their land without feeling too guilty.

This was the kind of world into which Sarah Winnemucca was born. She was a Paiute. The Paiutes lived in what is now called Nevada. Her grandfather Captain Truckee was an important person in the Paiute Nation. Her father was called Old Winnemucca, and he was a chief. Sarah's given name was Thocmetony, or Shell Flower.

By the time Shell Flower was an adult, she had fought in battle beside her father and uncle. She had seen her people executed in cold blood by whites and lied to by the government. She had also gone to a Catholic school and been kicked out because white parents didn't want their daughters in school with a "savage."

What these parents didn't know was that Shell Flower had mastered English and would go much further in life than any of their children. By the time she was twenty-two, she was considered to be the "chief" of the Paiutes by the U.S. government. Because of her language skills, she became the person the government turned to in order to settle disputes between her people and the white colonists.

She was called Princess Winnemucca by the newspapers. She would become one of the most famous American Indian women in history. She fought for all American Indian people. In all her roles—scout for the U.S. Army, diplomat, Paiute representative—she tried to get civil rights for her people.

When these campaigns did not succeed, she took her battle to the lecture halls. Sarah Winnemucca (the name she went by later in life) toured the country, speaking to large groups of mainly white people. She spoke about what the government had done and what it was currently doing to American Indians: putting them on reservations; stealing their land, their cattle, their buffalo, their water; and ignoring their complaints.

Against all odds, and in a time and a place dominated by violent men, Sarah Winnemucca was not afraid to stand up for what she knew was right. Though Sarah Winnemucca did not achieve everything she set out to achieve, and was underappreciated during her lifetime, no one has been a greater warrior in the American Indian struggle for fair treatment.

Carry A. Nation

[1846–1911] ★ *Temperance Activist*

Carry Nation was as big as the nation. She was six feet tall and weighed one hundred and eighty pounds. That's BIG!

When Carry Nation walked into a saloon, the men knew they had better get out of the way. They knew what she was fixing to do. She was fixing to bust up the place with her hatchet. That's because Carry Nation hated alcohol and the men who drank it. So she just walked into saloons and broke all the liquor bottles and shattered the mirrors behind the bars.

You see, her first husband was a drunk. On the day of their wedding, he got so drunk, he could barely pronounce the vows. She left him before long. Six months later he died from drinking too much.

By the time this happened, Carry was already very religious. So, after marrying a preacher, she didn't take long to figure out her life's mission: religious crusade against alcohol. All that was needed, Carry already had: a strong, domineering personality—with a side order of eccentricity.

For instance, she would walk down the street of Medicine Lodge, Kansas, armed with an umbrella that had a sharpened point. She would wave this umbrella at random people she believed to be sinners—while delivering short sermons against the evils of drinking and smoking. Back home she'd lock herself in the basement and wait for visions.

Her crusade against alcohol didn't get very far until 1880. That year, Carry came up with the brilliant idea that would make her famous: impromptu prayer meetings held in saloons. She led a group of religious wives into an illegal drinking establishment called Durst's Joint. Right there, in front of all the drunken cowboys and husbands, she and the other church ladies got down on their knees and started singing hymns. It worked! Those drunkards were knocking one another over trying to get out.

Her personal crusade then joined forces with a national movement called temperance. The purpose of the temperance movement was to shut down all the bars in America and to make alcohol illegal. It was the model for the Prohibition movement of the 1920s and '30s.

Carry Nation was probably the most famous leader of the temperance movement. That's because her methods were so extreme—and so effective. All over Kansas, she shut down saloon after saloon using prayers, bricks, hatchets, billiard balls, and the element of surprise. She didn't care about getting arrested. Her time in jail just won her more publicity and sympathy for her crusade.

Drinking was a big part of what made the West wild. It's odd that someone as wild as Carry Nation helped to tame the West. It must be noted, though, that she didn't "carry a nation" as she had planned. The saloons, over time, reopened. But it must also be said that Carry Nation did provide a way for Western wives to fight the rowdiness of their drunken husbands. She fought fire with fire (and brimstone).

Mary Ellen Pleasant

[1814–1904] ★ *Businesswoman*

Was she a freedom fighter? Was she a tycoon? Was she a voodoo queen? Or was she just a person people liked to talk about?

Mary Ellen Pleasant was a very unusual lady. As with Calamity Jane, a lot of mystery surrounds her story. Unlike Calamity Jane, she did her best to keep her story secret. Here's what is known.

Mary Pleasant was an ex-slave who was light skinned enough to pass for a white person. This helped her a lot when she moved to San Francisco during the gold rush era in 1850. No one knew she was African American. If they had, they would have treated her unfairly.

Instead, she gained entry into high society. She opened a boardinghouse where all the richest businessmen dined. Soon she became known as the best cook in San Francisco.

She talked to these businessmen and won their trust. Around her, they talked about the best places to invest money. She listened to them (sometimes from behind a closed door), and before you knew it, she was rich!

With her plentiful money, Mary Pleasant built a mansion, where she lived with friends. This incredible structure came to be known as The House of Mystery. It was filled with hidden stairways, secret spaces behind bookcases, entrances nobody knew about. To this day, no one really knows what went on there or why. The rumor was that Mary held voodoo rituals there. In the local newspapers, she was called the Voodoo Queen.

But the voodoo talk was only rumor. Had there been proof that she actually did the things of which she was accused (including murder), she would have gone to jail.

More likely than not, the Voodoo Queen label was just the newspapers' way of dismissing all of her success. In 1865, after the Civil War was over, she revealed her identity as an African American. She sued the city for discrimination on their cable cars—and she won. After that, San Francisco's high society was furious. They didn't care how much money she had. She was a black woman, an ex-slave, and she would never really be one of them.

Little did most San Franciscans know that during all those years she had passed as white, she had been secretly providing the last station on the Underground Railroad for most of the slaves who made it to San Francisco. She was responsible for many of the first black settlers in California. She gave them freedom, jobs, and shelter.

In her own sly way, Mary Ellen Pleasant was perhaps the most powerful woman of the Wild West.

The-Other-Magpie

[mid-1800s] ★ Woman Warrior

The-Other-Magpie was a famous woman warrior of the Crow tribe. The Crows lived in Montana before it was called Montana. They did a lot of fighting back in the days of the Wild West, mainly with other tribes such as the Sioux, the Cheyenne, and the Lakota.

When The-Other-Magpie went into battle, she was fierce looking. She wore a wild outfit with a stuffed woodpecker on her head—and her head was painted yellow. In other words, not too many people tangled with her.

Well, after The-Other-Magpie's brother had been killed by a member of the nearby Lakota tribe, she decided to go into battle against some Lakotas.

Luckily for The-Other-Magpie she wasn't alone. There were several other Crow warriors who came, too, including her good friend Finds-Them-and-Kills-Them.

The-Other-Magpie and Finds-Them-and-Kills-Them were just riding along singing, as they always did before battle, when they saw it: a line of Lakotas, stretched across the horizon, on horseback. It was at a place called Rosebud.

Finds-Them-and-Kills-Them swung into action, shooting the first Lakota she saw. Meanwhile, The-Other-Magpie stood near a wounded Crow warrior and waved her coupstick at a charging Lakota. The coupstick was a long weapon that had a feather on the end and was said to have magical powers. All The-Other-Magpie had to do was wave it and the Lakota turned and ran.

The Crows won the battle, and The-Other-Magpie rode back into the Crow village on her black horse. She was waving the scalp of a Lakota she had killed.

This is the only story about The-Other-Magpie that has been written down. It was told by the Crow medicine woman Pretty Shield long after the Wild West was over. There are many stories of American Indians that will never be known by most people because they were not written down. Who knows how many warrior women there may have been?

Nellie Cashman

[1850–1925] ★ *Adventurer and Philanthropist*

Nellie Cashman loved adventure. And she loved gold and silver. She traveled all over the Wild West, through snowy mountain passes and through hot deserts, to mine for silver and gold.

However, she didn't strike it rich in the mines. Nope, she found fame and fortune in the kitchen. By the age of twenty-five, this Irish emigrant had forged quite a reputation as a cook. She ran a popular boardinghouse for miners in the snowy mountains of British Columbia, Canada, up toward Alaska.

Here, Nellie had her first life-threatening adventure. The year was 1875. It was wintertime. A large group of prospectors had gotten stuck in a blizzard in the mountains miles and miles north of Victoria, the city where Nellie spent her winters. When she caught wind of the situation, she got out her snowshoes and food supplies and headed into the treacherous mountains.

The trip took weeks and weeks. The snow came down and down. A rescue team of soldiers was sent after Nellie. By the time the rescue team found her, it was the rescue team who needed Nellie's help. She fed the soldiers at her campfire and sent them packing the next morning. A couple of mornings later, she woke up in a snowdrift. She just shook off the snow and kept going. After eleven weeks, she finally found the abandoned miners, shivering and sick. Icicles hung from their grizzled beards. Nellie nursed the men back to health.

No Western woman or man had ever shown such daring and heroism in a blizzard. And no woman had ever run a business by herself in such frozen, remote country.

Three years later, Nellie was doing more or less the same thing in the hottest, driest place in the West: Arizona. Again there were miners to feed and money to be made. The silver mines were attracting all sorts of fortune seekers to the Tucson area, so Nellie opened a steak house there called Delmonico's. It went on to become the most famous restaurant in the Wild West.

Near Tucson there is a little town called Tombstone. In the 1880s, lots of people moved there because of the silver mines on the edge of town. As it turns out, Tombstone was well named. There, many desperadoes met their ends in unmarked graves on Boot Hill, the cemetery for outlaws.

Tombstone is the town where Nellie Cashman earned most of her fame. In 1880, she moved right in, opened a general store, a shoe store, and two restaurants, and made enough money to build a church and bankroll a hospital association and Tombstone's first musical comedy show.

She fed poor people, took in orphans, and protected the innocent, which is how she got her nickname, the Angel of Tombstone. But being an adventurer, Nellie couldn't just retire into angel-hood. The Wild West's last outpost was in the Yukon Territory. When the big Klondike gold rush of 1897 arrived, Nellie Cashman, forty-seven years old, had not given up. She was still panning for gold and making daring missions into the great unknown.

Long after the Wild West was over and she was seventy-four years old, Nellie Cashman drove a team of huskies 750 miles across the Arctic Circle—750 miles! You can take the wild woman out of the Wild West—but not vice versa.

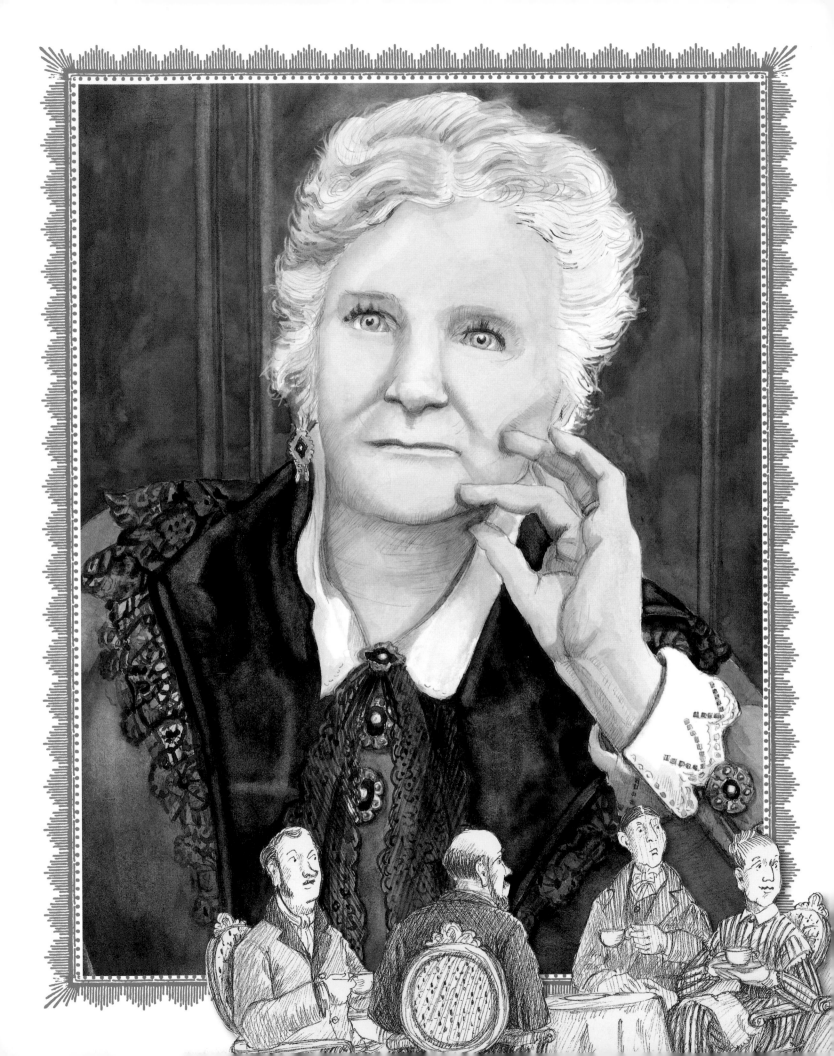

Esther Hobart McQuigg Slack Morris

[1814–1902] ★ *Activist and Judge*

Esther Hobart McQuigg Slack Morris had this tea party. Only it wasn't just a tea party. For one thing, it took place in Wyoming, where folks didn't drink all that much tea. She had the party in 1869, and she invited two important politicians who were running for a state legislative office.

Ms. Morris had a plan in mind. She wanted to get these two rivals all comfortable in her parlor. Then when they least suspected it, she would tell them her ideas. Or, actually, it was just one idea: women should be allowed to vote.

At that time, no woman in the world had ever voted. There was a political movement then in America called women's suffrage. Its purpose was to get women the right to vote.

Without ever giving a speech or writing a book, Esther Morris was one of the most important suffragists. This tea party was what drop-kicked her into the history books.

Setting down her teacup, Morris turned to the Democratic candidate, Colonel Bright. She asked him point-blank if he would give women the vote if elected. "Well . . . yes, of course!" he said, or something to that effect. And so, of course, the Republican candidate had to say he also would give women the vote. Both candidates had, basically, given their word to Morris in front of a lot of important local people.

Bright got elected and did introduce a bill giving women the right to vote. Ultimately, after much stalling and resistance, this bill passed! On December 10, 1869, the Wyoming Territory became the first place in the world where women could vote.

Wyoming women owed a lot to Esther Morris. She was a very forceful, articulate woman. It didn't hurt that she stood six feet tall and weighed one hundred and eighty pounds. She almost always got her way.

For instance, in 1870, Morris was elected judge of South Pass City. She was the first female judge in history! And to think, the first place in the whole world to elect a female judge was a small town in Wyoming. Then again, where better than in the Wild West to break with tradition!

✳ Wild West Time Line ✳

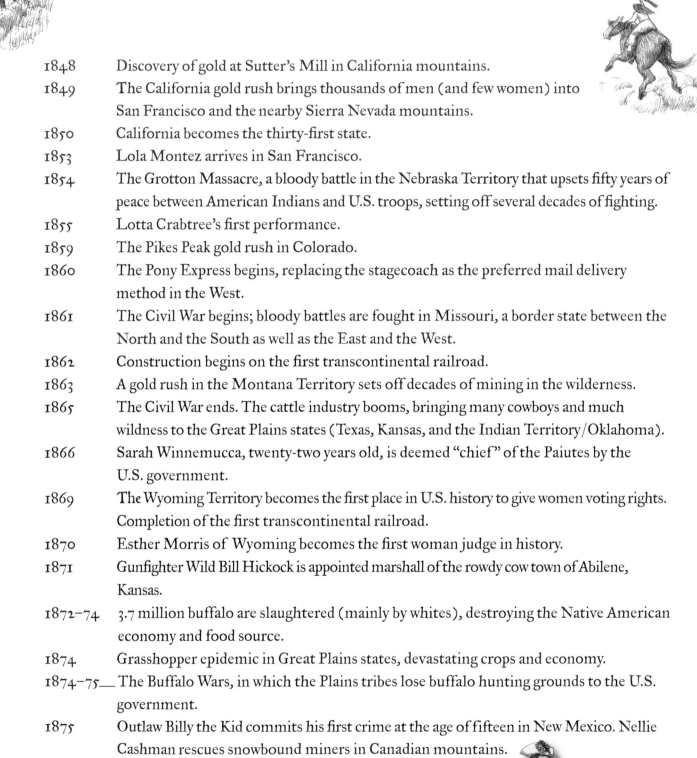

1848	Discovery of gold at Sutter's Mill in California mountains.
1849	The California gold rush brings thousands of men (and few women) into San Francisco and the nearby Sierra Nevada mountains.
1850	California becomes the thirty-first state.
1853	Lola Montez arrives in San Francisco.
1854	The Grotton Massacre, a bloody battle in the Nebraska Territory that upsets fifty years of peace between American Indians and U.S. troops, setting off several decades of fighting.
1855	Lotta Crabtree's first performance.
1859	The Pikes Peak gold rush in Colorado.
1860	The Pony Express begins, replacing the stagecoach as the preferred mail delivery method in the West.
1861	The Civil War begins; bloody battles are fought in Missouri, a border state between the North and the South as well as the East and the West.
1862	Construction begins on the first transcontinental railroad.
1863	A gold rush in the Montana Territory sets off decades of mining in the wilderness.
1865	The Civil War ends. The cattle industry booms, bringing many cowboys and much wildness to the Great Plains states (Texas, Kansas, and the Indian Territory/Oklahoma).
1866	Sarah Winnemucca, twenty-two years old, is deemed "chief" of the Paiutes by the U.S. government.
1869	The Wyoming Territory becomes the first place in U.S. history to give women voting rights. Completion of the first transcontinental railroad.
1870	Esther Morris of Wyoming becomes the first woman judge in history.
1871	Gunfighter Wild Bill Hickock is appointed marshall of the rowdy cow town of Abilene, Kansas.
1872–74	3.7 million buffalo are slaughtered (mainly by whites), destroying the Native American economy and food source.
1874	Grasshopper epidemic in Great Plains states, devastating crops and economy.
1874–75	The Buffalo Wars, in which the Plains tribes lose buffalo hunting grounds to the U.S. government.
1875	Outlaw Billy the Kid commits his first crime at the age of fifteen in New Mexico. Nellie Cashman rescues snowbound miners in Canadian mountains.

1876	Battle of Little Bighorn, in which U.S. General Custer loses to Crazy Horse in the greatest of all Native American war victories. Wild Bill Hickock is gunned down in a Deadwood saloon. Gunfighters Wyatt Earp and Bat Masterson are appointed assistant marshals of Dodge City, Kansas.
1877	Silver is discovered near Tombstone, Arizona, one of the last boomtowns in the Wild West.
1880	First Alaskan gold rush in Juneau.
1881	Shoot-out at the O.K. Corral in Tombstone, Arizona, between Wyatt Earp and the Ike Clanton gang. Carry Nation's first hymn-singing visit to a saloon in Medicine Lodge, Kansas. Billy the Kid is shot in his sleep by a lawman in New Mexico.
1882	Outlaw Jesse James is gunned down in his own house. Wyatt Earp leaves Tombstone amid talk of his potential arrest. Outlaw Roy Bean is appointed judge of Langtry, Texas, where he is saloon keeper, mayor, judge, executioner, and creator of "Law West of the Pecos." Belle Starr is put in jail for stealing horses.
1883	Debut of Buffalo Bill's Wild West Show.
1886	First major gold strike in the Yukon Territory, starting another gold rush. Apache warrior Geronimo surrenders to the U.S. Army and is imprisoned.
1886–87	End of the great cattle drives across the West because of drought, bankruptcies, and the arrival of sheep.
1889	The Hole-in-the-Wall gang (or "Wild Bunch") commits its first bank robbery in Denver, Colorado.
1889–92	Johnson County cattle range wars occur in the Wyoming Territory between local ranchers and gunslingers hired by outside businessmen.
1890	The Battle of Wounded Knee, the last of the Indian wars—a massacre of American Indians by U.S. troops.
1891	Native American leader Sarah Winnemucca dies poor and despised in the town named after her father: Winnemucca, Nevada.
1892	Mary Fields becomes the first woman to drive a stagecoach for the U.S. Postal Service (and its second female employee). The outlaw Dalton gang is gunned down during a bank robbery attempt in Coffeyville, Kansas.
1893	The last transcontinental line, the Great Northern Railway, is completed.
1895	Outlaw John Wesley Hardin is gunned down in an El Paso, Texas, saloon.
1897	Klondike gold rush begins.
1898	Between 30,000 and 40,000 people "stampede" to the Klondike (between Canada and Alaska), where some die in avalanches and many turn back. The last Alaskan gold rush in Nome.

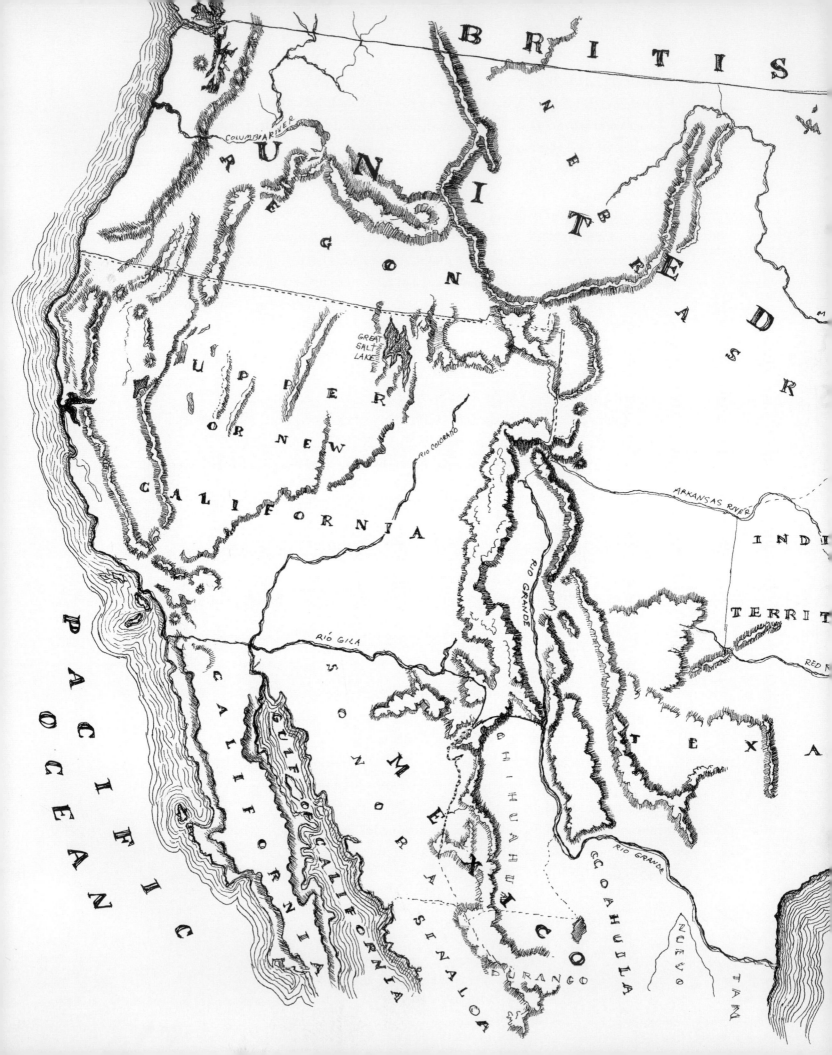

❋ Bibliography ❋

Aikman, Duncan. *Calamity Jane and the Lady Wildcats*. Lincoln, Nebraska: The University of Nebraska Press, 1987.

Bataille, Gretchen M., ed. *Native American Women: A Biographical Dictionary*. New York: Garland Publishing, 1993.

Brown, Dee. *Gentle Tamers: Women of the Old Wild West*. Lincoln, Nebraska: The University of Nebraska Press, 1981.

Canary, Martha Jane. *The Life and Adventures of Calamity Jane by Herself*. Lincoln, Nebraska: The University of Nebraska Press, 1987.

Dempsey, David, with Raymond P. Baldwin. *The Triumphs and Trials of Lotta Crabtree*. New York: William Morrow & Company, 1968.

Emmett, Chris. *Fort Union and the Winning of the Southwest*. Norman, Oklahoma: The University of Oklahoma Press, 1965.

Foley, Doris. *The Divine Eccentric: Lola Montez and the Newspapers*. Los Angeles: Westernlore Press, 1969.

Holdredge, Helen. *Mammy Pleasant*. New York: G. P. Putnam's Sons, 1953.

———. *The Woman in Black: The Life of Lola Montez*. New York: G. P. Putnam's Sons, 1953.

Horan, James David. *Desperate Women*. New York: Bonanza Books, 1952.

James, Edward T. *Notable American Women: A Biographical Dictionary, 1607–1950*. Cambridge, Massachusetts: Harvard University Press, 1971.

Katz, William Loren. *Black Women of the Old West*. New York: Atheneum Books for Young Readers, 1995.

Levine, Ellen. *Ready, Aim, Fire!: The Real Adventures of Annie Oakley*. New York: Scholastic Press, 1989.

Linderman, Frank B. *Pretty Shield: Medicine Woman of the Crows*. New York: The John Day Company, 1972.

McLoughlin, Dennis. *Wild and Woolly: An Encyclopedia of the Old West*. New York: Doubleday, 1975.

Miller, Robert. *Reflections of a Black Cowboy*. New York: Simon & Schuster, 1991.

Peavy, Linda, and Ursula Smith. *Pioneer Women: The Lives of Women on the Frontier*. New York: Smithmark Publishers, 1996.

Phillips, Charles, and Alan Axelrod, eds. *Encyclopedia of the American West*, Volume 4. New York: Simon & Schuster, 1997.

Roach, Joyce Gibson. *The Cowgirls*. Denton, Texas: The University of North Texas Press, 1990.

Sinnot, Susan. *Extraordinary Hispanic Americans*. Chicago: Children's Press, 1991.

Stiller, Richard. *Queen of the Populists: The Story of Mary Elizabeth Lease*. New York: T. Y. Crowell Co., 1970.

Tardiff, Joseph C., and L. Mabunda, eds. *Dictionary of Hispanic Biography*. Detroit, Michigan: Gale Research, Inc., 1996.

Walker, Paul Robert. *Trail of the Wild West… Rediscovering the American Frontier*. Washington, D.C.: National Geographic Society, 1997.

Western Writers of America. *The Women Who Made the West*. New York: Doubleday, 1980.

Illustrator's note:

I was struck by the independence, courage, and tenacity of these wild women and am grateful for the honor of illustrating them. All but two portraits were taken directly from photographic reference. In some cases, the information was fuzzy or vague at best, and I resorted to models to help me re-create the pose. There are no known photographs of either The-Other-Magpie or La Tules, though there is a black-and-white engraving of the latter from a *Harper's Weekly* magazine of 1854. Artistic license in hand, I posed models for both of these women and adjusted their features and clothing to those appropriate for the time period.

The map was referenced from a reproduction of the original drawn by G. W. Colton, and published by J. H. Colton, New York, 1850.